HEY CANADA!

By Vivien Bowers   Illustrated by **Milan Pavlovic**

TUNDRA BOOKS

For Jelena, who shares her dreams with me. — M.P.

Published in Canada by Tundra Books,
75 Sherbourne Street, Toronto, Ontario M5A 2P9
Published in the United States by Tundra Books of Northern New York,
P.O. Box 1030, Plattsburgh, New York 12901

Library of Congress Control Number: 2011923470

Library and Archives Canada Cataloguing in Publication
Bowers, Vivien, 1951-
Hey Canada! / by Vivien Bowers ; illustrated by Milan Pavlovic.

ISBN 978-1-77049-255-4

1. Canada--Description and travel--Juvenile literature.
2. Canada--Juvenile literature. I. Pavlovic, Milan II. Title.

FC58.B682 2012   j917.104   C2011-901454-8

We acknowledge the financial support of the Government of Canada through the Book Publishing Industry
Development Program (BPIDP) and that of the Government of Ontario through the Ontario Media Development
Corporation's Ontario Book Initiative. We further acknowledge the support of the Canada Council for the Arts
and the Ontario Arts Council for our publishing program.

ONTARIO ARTS COUNCIL
CONSEIL DES ARTS DE L'ONTARIO

Printed and bound in China

1 2 3 4 5 6   17 16 15 14 13 12

TABLE OF CONTENTS

Get Ready, Canada. We're Coming   4

The Big Picture:
Canada's Provinces and Territories   6

Newfoundland and Labrador   8

Nova Scotia   11

Prince Edward Island   16

New Brunswick   18

Quebec   21

Ontario   26

Manitoba   33

Saskatchewan   38

Alberta   41

British Columbia   46

Yukon   52

Northwest Territories   56

Nunavut   61

Trip's End   64

The Big Picture: This Land of Ours   66

Photography Credits   69

Index   70

GET READY, CANADA. WE'RE COMING

I'm Alice, nine years old, reporting from the backseat of the car. I'm writing this blog on Gran's netbook. My cousin Cal is sitting up front because he gets carsick. He's eight. Gran is driving.

The trip is her idea. She says she wants to do a road trip with her grandkids before she's old and creaky. On the back of her car she's glued a bumper sticker: "CANADA – COAST TO COAST TO COAST!" It's next to her other bumper sticker: "CAUTION: DRIVER MAY BE SINGING." (True, unfortunately.)

The heroes of this story.

We'll be starting in St. John's, the capital city of Newfoundland and Labrador. The plan is to drive through every province and territory in Canada, camping along the way. We'll visit every capital city. But Gran says we should be open to unexpected detours. We should welcome surprises on this trip.

RULES FOR WELL-BEHAVED GRANDCHILDREN

1. No whining.
2. No asking "Are we there yet?" (If you do, I will start to sing opera. Loudly.)
3. No wildlife in the car. ↙ Except hamsters.
4. Feed the driver cookies.

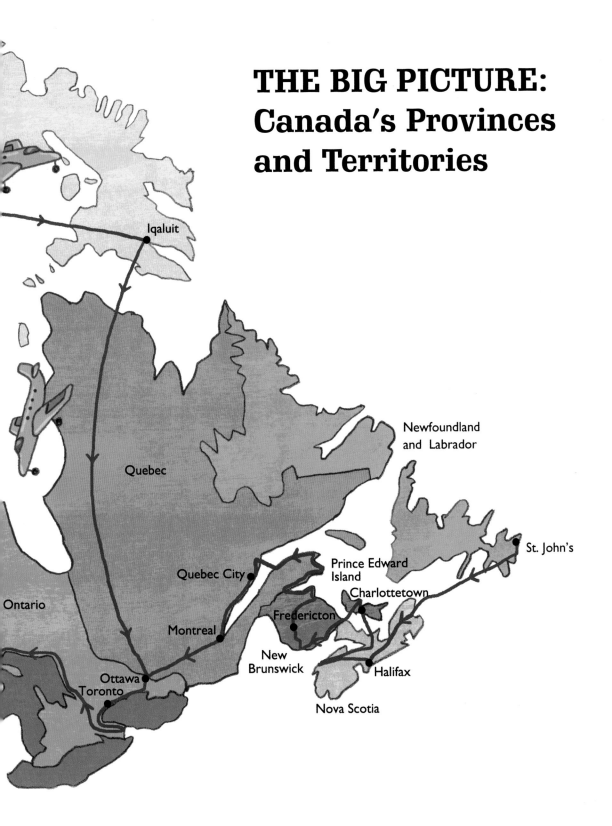

THE BIG PICTURE:
Canada's Provinces and Territories

Iqaluit

Newfoundland
and Labrador

Quebec

St. John's

Quebec City

Prince Edward
Island

Charlottetown

Ontario

Fredericton

Montreal

New
Brunswick

Halifax

Ottawa
Toronto

Nova Scotia

Pitcher Plant

This province needs a shorter nickname. Maybe..."Newfdor"!

NEWFOUNDLAND AND LABRADOR
On Your Mark, Get Set...

Puffin

St. John's

Hello from "The Rock." Gran says that's the real nickname for Newfoundland.

We started our day at Cape Spear. It's the farthest east you can go in North America. Any farther east and we'd fall into the Atlantic Ocean. (Cal nearly did – he was trying to taste it.)

St. John's

From the top of Signal Hill we looked way down on the Narrows, the channel leading into St. John's Harbour. We wished we had cannonballs. When Britain and France were fighting here long ago, they dropped cannonballs onto each other's ships from this high point.

Cal pretended *he* was going to cannonball into the Narrows! Gran just shrugged. So he didn't.

St. John's is the capital city of Newfoundland and Labrador. (Note to self: don't confuse this St. John's with Saint John in New Brunswick.) Gran says St. John's is the oldest city in Canada, almost five hundred years old.

"Older than you!" I said.

"Watch it," said Gran. "It's a long walk across Canada."

Gran says people came here from Europe to fish for cod. There were so many fish they could be scooped up in baskets. The cod were salted and dried in the sun.

"Blech!" said Cal. He hates fish.

Gran said the cod are almost all gone now. Otherwise, we could have tried eating cod cheeks – a special treat.

"No comment," said Cal.

🔍 FIND IT!

Gran gave us this list of things to find in Newfoundland. We can't leave the province until we see them all!

- Cod
- Moose
- Atlantic Ocean – just a taste
- Iceberg
- Puffin

Iceberg Alert!

Icebergs like this one float along the coast. They've broken off from glaciers in the Arctic. Cal says I should tell you that the ice can be ten thousand years old. He says icebergs can be as big as skyscrapers, and that seven-eighths of an iceberg is hidden under the water. (Gran calls Cal our Official Fact Dispenser.)

Norsemen Were Here

L'Anse aux Meadows (how to say it: "Lan-so meh-dows") is on the northern tip of Newfoundland. At one time, Norsemen from Greenland lived here. That was a thousand years ago. They didn't stay long, but they left stuff behind. That's how we know that they were here – we've dug it up.

Just across the channel is Labrador, the other part of this province. We don't have time to go there this trip. Gran says there aren't many roads there anyway. Lots of caribou and mosquitoes. There's a place called Red Bay that was "The Whaling Capital of the World" about 450 years ago. Luckily for the whales, it no longer is. You can dive underwater there and find sunken whaling ships.

Big Nose

We pulled over to say hi to a moose along the highway. He ignored us – how rude! Apparently moose weigh as much as three refrigerators (thanks to Cal, the Official Fact Dispenser, for that). Moose look like cartoon animals. They have big noses and dangling hair under their chins. Cal said that dangly, hairy skin under their chin is called a dewlap.

↖ Dewlap

"Oh," said Gran. "I thought it was a 'moose-tache.'"

Puffin

Puff, puff, puff. We saw puffins, Newfdor's provincial bird! They were launching off sea cliffs, catching fish. At first I thought they were parrots.

"Nope," said Gran. "That ain't nuffin' but a puffin."

This might be a long trip across Canada.

 CAL'S TWEET

Newfoundland's official flower, the pitcher plant, eats insects. A fact. Bugs get trapped inside the flower cup and drown in rainwater.

NOVA SCOTIA
...e Bagpipes!

Osprey

Halifax

dancing. Gran's foot was tapping to the beat. Cal tried standing on Gran's foot. When she started dancing a jig, he fell off.

Our cross-Canada trip may have a music delay. Gran is having too much fun to leave the ceilidh.

Driving the Cabot Trail

We are driving around Cape Breton Island – up and down, twisting and turning . . . Cal says he's going to get carsick. Oh, great.

We're on Cape Breton Island, at the north end of Nova Scotia. It's hilly and windy. Waves crash against sea cliffs.

We went to a ceilidh (how to say it: "kay-lay"). It's a party with music and

🔍 FIND IT!

- Piece of coal
- British fort with cannons
- Ceilidh
- Something tartan

We stopped at a trail to some sea cliffs. Gran grabbed her binocs (binoculars) and went looking for birds.

"The hunt is on for guillemots." (How to say it: "gull-i-mot.") She said, "They have red feet. They nest on rocky cliffs here." Cal and I looked at each other, shrugged, and followed.

Down in the Coal Mine

We went underground into a coal mine.

"What if the tunnel collapses?" I asked.

Gran looked at me in disbelief. "Would I put you in danger?"

"Or what if gas explodes in the mine?"

"Alice, I promise: nobody will explode today," Gran said.

A retired miner took us down into the dark mine. He said it was the first time he'd had a hamster on his tour. The mine's tunnels stretch way out under the sea. We wore hard hats with lights on them. We learned about the pit ponies that used to pull carts of coal through the mine. Those poor ponies never saw sunlight.

Halifax

Reporting from Nova Scotia's capital city. We're at the Citadel. It's a British fort that was built to defend Halifax against French attackers. It's on a hill overlooking the city. The guards wear tartan kilts and furry hats that look like they would make heads feel hot. We watched the soldiers fire a cannon. There was a big bang and lots of smoke.

"My ears hurt," said Gran. "Let's go explore the harbor."

"We can't!" said Cal. "The French might attack. We have to stay here and defend Halifax!"

Gran sighed. "Let's just share it with the French," she said.

Halifax Harbour

The harbor is in the oldest part of Halifax. At the Privateers' Warehouse, we learned about the Halifax pirates here two hundred years ago. Actually, they were privateers, not pirates. They had permission from King George III to raid enemy ships. They gave some of their booty to His Majesty, and kept the rest. Cal was disappointed that they didn't wear eye patches, like proper pirates.

Digby

At Digby, Gran and I ate scallops for lunch. Gran ate Cal's scallops, too. He says he's allergic. Then we spent the afternoon on the sandy beach collecting scallop shells. I'm going to make a mobile with them. Cal says it will stink. He might be right. The smell is already coming through the plastic bag.

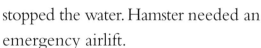

Cal and I built this amazing sand fort for Hamster. The tide came in, closer and closer. It was going to wreck our fort! We built barricades. We dug a moat. Nothing stopped the water. Hamster needed an emergency airlift.

Port-Royal

Port-Royal is the first place where people from Europe settled in Canada. A French explorer named Samuel de Champlain came here with his men in 1605. That was more than four hundred years ago. You couldn't convince me to

WOULD YOU LIKE TO TRY SOME TAIL OF A BEAVER?

SAMUEL DE CHAMPLAIN

live at Port-Royal back then – it wasn't very comfy. The pioneers ate the tails of beavers and the noses of moose! Sometimes they got a disease called scurvy and their teeth fell out. The winters were long and miserable. Champlain had a good idea, though. He started a club, and the men took turns serving feasts. That cheered them up.

But Port-Royal was captured by English soldiers. Then the French took it back again. Then English, then French. Finally, in 1710, the British got it for keeps.

Hamster Update

We bought Hamster a lobster pot (a trap) to use for a cage. Cal made an adventure playground inside it, using a cardboard tube, driftwood, and a fishing float we found on the beach. Hamster seems to like it. He's snoozing in there somewhere. Lobsters enter here.

 CAL'S TWEET

Tried eating haggis. Big mistake. Made from sheep's heart, lungs, and liver – and oatmeal. Tastes like dog food.

Good-bye

We're leaving Nova Scotia now. Gran is driving, singing a song called "Farewell to Nova Scotia." She's singing quietly because Cal is asleep in the passenger seat, his mouth hanging open. I took a photo. It might be useful later.

Then I snuggled into my sleeping bag nest and looked out the window. "Farewell to Nova Scotia, the sea-bound coast," sang Gran.

I closed my eyes to listen . . .

"Gotcha!" said Cal, holding up his camera. "You do too snore!"

PRINCE EDWARD ISLAND
Red Sand Beaches

Blue Jay

Lady's Slipper

Charlottetown

Welcome to Prince Edward Island, also known as PEI, the teensiest province of Canada. We took the ferry from Nova Scotia to get here. Then we drove to Charlottetown, PEI's capital city.

Charlottetown – Where Canada Began

Our first stop was Founders' Hall. We were lucky to find it because Hamster has been chewing on the Charlottetown map. We aren't sure how he got out of his lobster pot.

"Plug the hole!" ordered Gran.

At Founders' Hall, we were welcomed by some Fathers and Ladies of Confed-eration dressed in very fancy clothes. The women wore dresses with enormous skirts that stuck out all around. That style was normal back in 1867, when Canada was founded.

"You could hide a lot of hamsters under one of those skirts," whispered Gran to Cal.

"Sh!" whispered Cal. Hamster was up his sleeve. Pets are probably not allowed in Founders' Hall. But Gran didn't want to leave Hamster in the hot car where he would eat more maps.

Founders' Hall is all about the men who founded Canada. They started working on the plan here, in Charlotte-town. We put on headphones and walked through The Time Travel Tunnel into the past. I learned how Canada began.

At first, the territory was a lot smaller. Only Nova Scotia, New Brunswick, Quebec, and Ontario agreed to join the new country. Later PEI did too, and all the other provinces and territories.

IT'S THE TRUTH!
(Cal's Factoid)

Why is PEI sand red? Because it's full of iron. When iron gets wet and rusts, it turns orangey-red.

Red Sand!

We turned red at the beach, but not from sunburn. Blame it on PEI's red sand. I lay on the warm beach and trickled sand through my fingers. PEI sand is beautiful. It has lots of different colors in it. We were joined on the beach by big, floppy-winged great blue herons.

Green Gables

Tour bus alert. A parking lot full of tour buses means it's a touristy spot, like Green Gables. This house was the home of Anne of Green Gables. She's a character in a famous storybook. Gran read the book when she was a girl, and now I'm reading it. Anne had red hair, and spelled her name with an *E*.

Each year, two hundred and fifty thousand tourists visit Anne's house.

That's funny, because Anne was never a real person. A lot of the visitors come from Japan. Anne of Green Gables is a legendary character there.

 CAL'S TWEET

PEI is famous for potatoes. More than 70 different kinds of spuds grow here!

Confederation Bridge

When we left PEI, we drove across Confederation Bridge. The bridge is thirteen kilometers (8 miles) long. There's a curve in the middle so drivers don't fall asleep. Gran said she didn't need the curve. She sings to stay awake.

"We wish you didn't," we said.

 **FIND IT!**

- Green Gables
- Confederation Bridge
- Potato
- Red sand

NEW BRUNSWICK
Covered Bridges & Big Tides

Black-Capped Chickadee

Purple Violet

Fredericton

"Let's find every single covered bridge in New Brunswick!" said Gran. "All sixty-five of them."

Covered bridges are a New Brunswick thing. The bridges have wooden roofs over them.

"I've a better plan," said Cal. "Let's watch Alice try to outrun the tide coming into the Bay of Fundy."

We visited Hopewell Cape at low tide. On the sandy beach, there are towering rocks, and trees grow out of them. The rocks are as high as four-storey buildings. At high tide, the water comes up almost to the tops of the rocks and they become little islands. We could see the high-tide line – way over our heads. I kept checking my watch, to make sure that we didn't stay on the beach too long!

Gran says I'm her Official Worrier. With me along, she doesn't have to worry about anything.

Bay of Fundy

The Bay of Fundy has the biggest tides in the world! Since the beach is flat, the tide comes a long way in. Sometimes it comes in faster than you can run.

🔍 **FIND IT!**

• Covered bridge
• Acadian flag
• Low tide
• Dulse

To Fredericton

We drove along the Saint John River this morning. Little cable ferries took us back and forth across the river.

In Fredericton, the capital city of this province, we explored the old part of town – the Garrison District. It's where British soldiers lived over two hundred years ago. We got to pretend to be soldiers and wear red tunics. The guard commander showed us how to march. He took us into the old guardhouse, where bad people were locked up. It was a nasty place. We promised not to be bad.

Kings Landing

Then we took a trip back in time to a village in the 1800s. Women wore long dresses and bonnets. The boys had trousers held up with suspenders. We rode around in a wagon pulled by a horse. It had bumpy wooden wheels. Cal thought someone should invent rubber tires.

A man who worked there told us that the villagers had been United Empire Loyalists. And he was dressed up to look like one. "I'm loyal to Britain!" he said. "Long live the king!"

He said that Loyalists escaped from United States and fled to Canada in the 1780s. The Americans didn't like them because the Loyalists were loyal to Britain.

The Americans were tired of Britain telling them what to do. Out with the British! So the Loyalists came to Canada. Lots of today's New Brunswick families are descendants of the Loyalists.

Gran plunked herself down to listen to some fiddle music. Cal and I went to churn butter.

At the Beach

We've driven in a big loop and now we're back on the east coast of New Brunswick. We spent all day at a huge national park with a long name.

"Kouchibouguac," said Gran. (How to say it: "Koo-shee-boo-gwak.")

"Yeah, that one," I said.

We hiked along the boardwalk to Kelly's Beach. It's a beach with sand dunes, and it never ends. I know, because we walked forever. Cal and I made fun of the sandpiper birds, copying their straight-legged strut along the edge of the water. Then Gran pointed out the terns swooping about (they look like seagulls), so we became terns. Around and around we turned.

"Enough, you birdbrains!" said Gran. "You're making me dizzy. Go swim!"

The water was warm in the lagoons. Luckily Cal remembered to take Hamster out of his pocket.

CAL'S TWEET

Avoid dulse, a seaweed snack eaten in New Brunswick. Salty, tastes like fish food. Proven fact: Hamster is not fond of dulse.

Acadia

We're in Acadia! The Acadians moved here in about 1760. That was after the British kicked them out of their homes in Nova Scotia.

At the Acadian Village, we found out what it was like to be Acadian long ago. We bought an Acadian flag that is now flying from our radio antenna.

The Acadians spoke French. That's why about one-third of New Brunswick people speaks French now.

QUEBEC
Parlez-Vous Français?

Blue Flag

Snowy Owl →

Quebec City

I was worried crossing the border into Quebec. I don't speak much French. As for Gran, she knows enough to ask a question – but not always enough to understand the answer. Not helpful.

I guess Cal is our best bet. He is in French Immersion at school. Gran gave him a French phrase book to study. So far he has learned that French-speaking cows say *meuh* instead of *moo*. That's only useful if we are talking to cows.

The Gaspé

We drove across the Gaspé Peninsula. It's the southern part of Quebec that sticks out into the Gulf of Saint Lawrence like a tongue.

"I can stick out my tongue, too," said Cal.

"Don't bother," said Gran.

We're camped tonight at the tip of the tongue, overlooking the ocean. From here we can see Rocher Percé (Pierced Rock) – a huge rock with a hole in it.

Île Bonaventure is a bird sanctuary. You get there by boat. Up close, it stinks like you wouldn't believe. A lot of the squawking birds are gannets. They nest on the cliffs and dive-bomb into the water. Sploosh! Then they come up with a mouthful of fish.

 **FIND IT!**

- Saint Lawrence River
- Baguette
- Fleur de lis
- Sign written in French

Along the Saint Lawrence River

We took a ferry across the mighty Saint Lawrence River. We waved to freighters going by. On the north side, we drove along the river to Tadoussac to look for whales. The water there is full of krill – tiny shrimp-like critters that these whales like to eat.

There were tons of whale-watching boats. Gran decided the whales had enough people bothering them, so we drove on to Charlevoix. There are stone houses and farms, and some crazy steep and zigzagging roads.

At a *boulangerie* (bakery) in Baie Saint-Paul, we bought a fresh baguette. A baguette is a long, skinny loaf of bread. It's perfect for bopping know-it-all cousins on the head.

While chewing on our baguette at a picnic table, we listened to the people around us speaking French. There are lots of artists in Baie Saint-Paul. If I decide to be an artist, I'll come and live here. And eat baguettes.

Quebec City

We're in a really old city surrounded by old stone walls. Quebec City is the capital of the province. (Having one Quebec inside another Quebec is confusing.) On the stone wall, there are cannons that we pretended to fire. Boom! (Gran ducked and covered her ears.)

From the Upper Town, we ran down to the Lower Town, where there's a maze of little streets. One of them is the narrowest street in North America! We took a shortcut down some stairs called Escalier Casse-Cou. That means "Breakneck Stairs." We flew down at breakneck speed. Gran was scared to look.

We thought this hotel, the Château Frontenac, looked like a castle. It's the most photographed hotel in the world. We met Santo, a huggable dog who lives at the hotel. His official title is Canine Ambassador. His job is to be adorable.

The Quebec symbol is a fleur-de-lis – a lily.

Montreal

Bienvenue a (welcome to) Montreal! Or, as the French say it, "Mo-ray-al." It's the second biggest city in Canada. Lots of people here speak French. Lots speak English. Lots speak other lan-guages. They figure it out.

Mont Royal

Gran likes to start a visit to a new place with a bird's-eye view. So we climbed a mighty mountain – Mont Royal. It's in the middle of a big park. From the top, you can look down on the city.

Gran opened her backpack and pulled out lunch. She brought bagels with smoked meat from a deli. It's a Montreal specialty. Afterward, we begged for ice cream. It was a matter of life or death.

"To recover from our big climb up Mont Royal," said Cal.

"And to give us energy for the walk down," I said.

"Me too," Gran agreed.

Old Montreal

We took the underground Metro to Old Montreal. We walked around the narrow streets and checked out the old stone buildings.

"How come you like all this old stuff, Gran?" I asked.

Gran thought a bit. "I like seeing what it was like back then. It's like reading the first chapters of a story. The rest of the story makes more sense if you know how it all started."

I pondered that for a while.

"For instance, Montreal used to be an Iroquoian village called Hochelega. Then it was a fur-trading center called Ville-Marie. And then it grew into a city."

"Well, this old stuff gives me sore feet," said Cal. So we found a grassy park down by the river. Cal sat beside the pond and talked to the ducks until his feet recovered.

After supper, Gran said, "Let's go find some joie de vivre." She said there's lots in certain parts of Montreal. Turns out joie de vivre just means "enjoying life." People do that a lot in Montreal. It's like a big street party – lots of musicians and street performers. The joie de vivre goes on and on until really late at night.

Hamster Update

Hamster continues to escape. He chews through everything. Gran calls him Houdini (how to say it: "Who-dee-nee") after a famous escape artist. Cal is trying to train him.

Biodome

We went to a tropical rainforest. It's inside a huge dome called the Biodome! We saw monkeys, crocodiles, and poison arrow frogs. Cal's favorite was the capybara – the world's biggest rodent. My favorite? The little penguins sliding down the snow in the polar exhibit. They were hilarious.

Nearby was The Big O. It's a stadium that was built for the Olympic Games. A cable car goes up the slanty tower. The view is stupendous! Cal wouldn't know – he read his phrase book the whole time.

BATTLE ON THE PLAINS OF ABRAHAM
QUEBEC CITY, 1759

MORNING ON THE PLAINS OF ABRAHAM

THE PLAINS OF ABRAHAM TODAY...

ONTARIO
Loons and Great Lakes

White Trillium

Common Loon

Toronto

"Ontario is big!" I said, looking at the map as we crossed the border. "Sure is," said Gran. "Settle in."

Ottawa – Parliament Buildings

Canada's capital city. The Parliament buildings look very important! When you look close up, you can see that the walls inside and out are covered in carvings. We especially liked the funny make-believe creatures with their tongues sticking out. My neck is sore from looking up.

Very important people, like the prime minister, work in the Parliament buildings. They make laws and run the country. We peeked into the huge room where they meet. There's a big chair at the front, like a throne. That's the Speaker's chair. He or she wears a three-cornered black hat called a tricorn and is supposed to make sure that everyone behaves. Because of the hat, Cal thought the Speaker was a pirate.

Parliament is not sitting at the moment. So we couldn't watch our members of Parliament at work. Too bad, because Cal and I thought up some new laws they should make. All roads in Canada should be painted yellow and pink – that's one. Also, it should be illegal to sing opera.

"What does Parliament do when it's not sitting?" I asked Gran. "Does it

🔍 FIND IT!

- CN Tower
- Niagara Falls
- Great Lakes
- Parliament buildings
- Terry Fox statue
- Gigantic Canada goose

stand? Go for a walk? Have a snooze?"

"I can't hear you," said Gran. "I seem to have gone deaf."

Centennial Flame

This gas flame in front of the Parliament buildings burns forever. Around it are symbols of all the provinces and territories in Canada – all but Nunavut, anyway. Nunavut became a territory in 1999, too late to be included.

Ottawa Museums

Ottawa has many museums. For instance, a war museum, a nature museum, a science museum – even a postal museum.

"We can't do them all," said Cal.

We went to the Museum of Civili-zation, which has wiggly walls. In the Grand Hall, we found this overloaded canoe. I hope it doesn't tip over. The entire family of living beings is apparently in that canoe. We picked out Raven, Eagle, and Grizzly Bear. It was made by a Haida artist named Bill Reid. He said even he wasn't sure where the paddlers were headed.

We walked through the Canada Hall, which goes through a thousand years of Canadian history. Cal zoomed through his historical tour at warp speed, then spent the rest of the time going up and down the escalators. Gran took two hours for her tour. She came out looking bug-eyed.

"I need fresh air!" she said.

So we went exploring.

Around Ottawa

The Rideau Canal goes though Ottawa. It was built two hundred years ago. The canal used to be a sneaky water route for sending military supplies to Ottawa from Kingston. Now it's just used by boaters, and, in winter, it's the world's biggest skating rink.

We said hello to some statues in Ottawa. They are everywhere! For instance, in Hull, there's a statue of Rocket Richard, who was a star hockey player. Lots of prime ministers from the old days, too. There's another of the Famous Five women having a tea party outside the Parliament buildings. (They are famous because they helped change the rules so women could vote in Canada.) Gran sat down and joined them for tea.

I whispered a quiet hello at the Tomb of the Unknown Soldier. It's at the National War Memorial, near the Parliament buildings. Inside the tomb is a soldier who died in France in World War II. Nobody knows his name. He stands for all the Canadians who've died in wars. On Remembrance Day, November 11, people put poppies on his tomb.

Toronto

We're in Canada's biggest city. Ontario's capital city! The best way to see Toronto is from the top. So, up the CN Tower we went.

From the top, you can see south over Lake Ontario – one of the Great Lakes. On the other side, the city stretches inland as far as you can see.

Stepping onto the glass floor feels like walking on thin air. You can gaze straight down, down, down below your feet to what looks like toy cars driving on toy city streets. It's 112 stories down. Cal couldn't do it.

"It makes me feel woozy," he said. "I feel like I'm going to fall through."

"That's the fun of it," said Gran.

IT'S THE TRUTH!
(Cal's Factoid)

The CN Tower is 533.3 meters (1,815 feet, 5 inches) tall. It used to be the world's tallest tower until two countries – Dubai and China – built taller ones. At night, it is lit up in different colors, like red and white for Canada Day.

Around Toronto

Toronto has an underground subway. Gran got a subway map and gave it to Cal and me. "Figure it out," she said.

We figured out how to ride the subway to the ROM, the Royal Ontario Museum. It's a big museum with dinosaurs and a creepy Egyptian mummy. We also went on an extra subway ride to nowhere and back. That's because Cal didn't tell us when to get off.

We wandered around Kensington Market, where you can buy foods from all around the world. Lots of

smelly cheeses. Bins full of strange UFOs (Unidentified Food Objects). People in Toronto come from all over the world. Gran says that's what makes it so interesting.

Niagara Falls

So huge! So loud! So wet!

At Niagara Falls, we went on the Maid of the Mist boat. It goes right

up to the bottom of the Falls. The noise was thundering, and the spray got us soaked.

"Hang on to your hamsters!" yelled Gran as we pitched in the waves.

The Great Lakes

Lake Michigan is the only lake not in Canada. The border with the United States goes right through the middle of the other four. Lake Superior is the biggest.

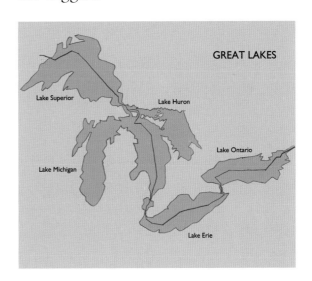

GREAT LAKES
Lake Superior
Lake Huron
Lake Ontario
Lake Michigan
Lake Erie

The Stanley Cup is displayed at Toronto's Hockey Hall of Fame.

TRUE NORTH KNIGHTS

IT'S THE TRUTH! (Cal's Factoid)

Freighters can travel all the way from the Atlantic Ocean up the Saint Lawrence River and through the Great Lakes to the other end. Each lake in the chain is a bit higher, so the ships need to go uphill. They use locks, but not the kind you put on doors. These locks are like water stairs.

HOW A LOCK WORKS:

1. Ship sails into the lock. Water-tight doors close in front and behind the ship.
2. Water pours into the lock. The ship floats higher and higher.
3. When the water is the same level as the canal ahead, the door in front of the ship opens. The ship sails out, continuing upstream. Bye-bye!

Niagara Escarpment

Cal loves to find out about stuff. It's like a disease he has. Gran keeps him busy figuring things out. Right now, Cal is figuring out about the Niagara Escarpment. It's a long ridge of rock that crosses southern Ontario. All along it, there are cliffs and waterfalls (especially at Niagara Falls). Most of Ontario is flat, so the escarpment stands out. Cal says that once upon a time it was the edge of a huge shallow sea.

We're going to hike the Niagara Escarpment. There's a trail all the way along.

"We can't do it all," said Cal. "It's 725 kilometers (450 miles) long."

"We'll just hike until we're so tired we drop dead," I suggested.

"We could sing along the way!" said Gran.

"Promise me you won't," I said.

Georgian Bay

We're camped on Georgian Bay, which is part of Lake Huron. We've found the longest sand beach! Gran says she needs some R & R (rest and relaxation) after our hike. Cal and I are here for S & S (swimming and splashing). Gran bought us blow-up animals to float on. I'm on a killer whale that likes to tip over. Cal has a polka-dotted dragon.

Tomorrow we're going to help Gran look for trumpeter swans at a marsh. Sounds rather noisy, I think. Then, back here for more S & S.

North of Lake Superior

We are somewhere along the shore of Lake Superior. Did I mention that Ontario was big? That it seems to go on forever? That we've been driving for days? And we're *still* in Ontario.

We stopped at Science North in Sudbury. At the museum, we met a porcupine named Quillan. Did you know that porcupines are shortsighted

and have thirty thousand quills? We also met a beaver named Drifter with only half a tail. Beavers are the largest rodents in Canada. Beavers can hold their breath for fifteen minutes underwater. Gran says don't try it.

Big Nickel

This nine-meter (30-foot) Big Nickel is in Sudbury, where there's a nickel mine. This particular nickel is made of steel, not nickel. It stands up to the weather better.

Giant goose sighting in Wawa. Wawa is from the Ojibwa word "wewe," which means "wild goose." This goose was very tame. It let us walk up close.

Hamster Update

Hamster has vamoosed. Escaped again! We've pulled apart the car, looking for him. We never found him. Gran says she never knew a hamster could be so much trouble.

Canadian Shield

The highway goes on and on. Trees and rocks. And lakes. And bog.

"This is the Canadian Shield," said Gran.

"Is there a Canadian sword?" I asked.

"I can't hear you," said Gran.

I guess that means no.

"The Canadian Shield was covered by ice during the ice ages," said Cal.

"The ice scraped across the land. It scraped away the soil. When the ice melted, it left lots of lakes behind."

I yawned. "How far to the Manitoba border?" I asked.

"You've got the map," said Gran. "Figure it out."

I did. Still over six hundred kilometers (372 miles) to go. I'm going to settle in for a nap.

Terry Fox Statue

I woke up to say hello to Terry Fox.

Terry Fox lost one leg to cancer. Just the same, he started running across Canada to raise money for cancer research. He ran 5,373 kilometers (3,339 miles). Then his cancer came back, and he had to quit. His statue is at the spot where he had to stop his cross-country run. He died soon after. Now, millions of people do the Terry Fox Run each year to raise money. Cal and I ran in it last year. I walked up to Terry's statue and thanked him for trying so hard.

MANITOBA
Friendly, Flat

Prairie Crocus

Great Grey Owl →

Winnipeg

We drove by something very exciting yesterday – the halfway mark! It means that we are now halfway across Canada! Go, team, go!

We are definitely on the Prairies now. The land is "flat as a pancake," as Gran says. Fields of wheat wave in the wind. The road goes straight – someone must have used a ruler. You can see a long way when there aren't any trees or mountains in the way.

Winnipeg – The Forks

Gran decided we should start our Winnipeg visit at The Forks.

"Forks?" said Cal. "Why not spoons?"

It turns out that The Forks are where two rivers flow together – the Assiniboine and the Red. There's a busy park there. We watched jugglers throwing crazy things into the air. Along the River Walk, there were signs in three languages: English, French, and Cree. Gran said there's a French-speaking area of Winnipeg called St. Boniface. Also, many people in Winnipeg are First Nations Cree. And *we* three speak English! (Well, so do other people here.) So – three languages!

The walk ended at the Manitoba legislative buildings. The Golden Boy is on top of the roof. He's a statue covered

with real gold. He is carrying some wheat.

Inside are two life-size bison statues that are so heavy that movers had a hard time bringing them into the building without scratching the floors. So they waited until winter, flooded the floor with water, and let it freeze. Then they put the bison on slabs of ice cut from the Assiniboine River and slid them in. That's the story, anyhow.

The Mint

"What'll it be: the Manitoba Museum or the Royal Canadian Mint?" asked Gran the next morning.

"Which one has an escalator?" asked Cal.

"I vote for the Mint," I said. "Show me the money!"

The Mint is where they make Canadian coins – fifteen million a day! A machine cuts round disks out of a flat strip of metal, like cutting cookies out of cookie dough. Then they use a stamp to put the image onto the coins.

Gran learned a new word today – *numismatist*. It's someone who collects coins.

"It sounds like a magic spell," I said, waving a pretend magic wand at her. "Numismatist!"

Gran snatched up her imaginary wand, too. "Counterspell . . . let's see . . . Winnipegosis!"

"What's that?" asked Cal.

"It's a lake in Manitoba. There's a Lake Winnipeg and a Lake Winnipegosis."

"Cool!" he said. I could see him filing away those words into his brain, for later use.

Lake Winnepeg

Floodway

We drove across the Red River Floodway. It's a canal around the city of Winnipeg. The canal gates are opened when water in the Red River gets too high and threatens to flood the city. Some of the water goes into this floodway and takes a detour around the city. Otherwise people in Winnipeg would need boats to get to work.

Lower Fort Garry

We went to an old Hudson Bay Company trading post. It's on the Red River. From here, workers paddled boats loaded with beaver skins to Hudson Bay. That's over a thousand kilometers (621 miles) away. And sometimes the heavy boats had to be dragged overland. We saw a huge metal sculpture of men pulling a boat over a portage trail.

"I'd die," I said.

"Or at least whine," said Gran.

We used touchscreens to learn about the fur trade and the trading posts up north where First Nations trappers brought the beaver skins to trade for blankets and stuff. The skins were sent to Europe to turn into fancy hats. Every well-dressed gentleman had to have one. The beavers were almost wiped out. Cal thought the gentlemen should have worn tuques or ball caps instead.

These Red River carts were pulled by horses or oxen. They were the "trucks" of prairie life in the 1800s. Their big wheels could roll through mud and marsh. The carts could be floated across streams. One problem: they were made of wood tied together with leather, and they made an ear-piercing squeal.

Chasing Birds

"Enough with city life," said Gran the next morning. "I need birds." So we drove to a marsh in the country. It's a favorite bird stopover. We walked along the boardwalk. We saw some black birds with yellow heads. I asked Gran what they were called.

"Yellow-headed blackbirds," said Gran.

"What about the ones with red wings?"

"Red-winged blackbirds," said Gran.

I told her I thought they should have fancier names.

"Like scatterbrained dippletwitt," said Cal.

"You saw one of those?" I asked.

"Nope. Just made it up."

I might have to throw him in Lake Winnipegosis.

 **FIND IT!**

- Field of wheat
- A sign that's not English or French
- The Golden Boy
- A coin
- Hudson Bay fort

Riding Mountain National Park

Reporting from the backseat with a sore bum. Yesterday we went horseback riding. My first time on a horse! At first I was scared, but then I loved it. My horse was named Jake.

The horses walked single file on a trail. Jake kept trying to stop and eat grass, holding up traffic. Bad Jake!

Gran is on the lookout for a lynx. It's a big wildcat and she's never seen

Hamster Update

Houdini lives! Gran found a stash of sunflower seeds at the bottom of her book bag. And my package of sunflower seeds that I keep in the backseat has a hole nibbled in it. So now we have evidence, but where is that rodent hiding? Cal is figuring out a "Hamster Capture Plan."

one. They have been spotted in the park before. Last night, Cal told her he could hear one outside the tent. It was gone by the time she opened the bug netting and poked her head out.

At breakfast, he tried again. "Look, Gran! A lynx! Right behind you!"

She didn't even turn around. She just glared at him. Then she pointed her imaginary wand in his direction. "Numismatist! Turn my grandson into a toad!"

PADDLING WITH THE VOYAGEURS: IN THE DAYS OF THE FUR TRADE, TWO HUNDRED YEARS AGO.

THE VOYAGEURS CARRIED SUPPLIES TO TRADING POSTS IN THE WILDERNESS. THEY CAME BACK LOADED WITH FURS.

THE RIVERS WERE LIKE TODAY'S HIGHWAYS. THE VOYAGEURS COVERED BIG DISTANCES, PADDLING DAY AFTER DAY.

SOMETIMES THE CANOES HAD TO BE PORTAGED AROUND RAPIDS OR BETWEEN LAKES.

THEY ATE PEMMICAN — DRIED MEAT, FAT AND BERRIES POUNDED TOGETHER — AND SLEPT UNDER THEIR CANOES.

THE FURS WERE SHIPPED TO ENGLAND. THE HAIRS WERE CUT OFF, CHOPPED, CRUSHED, AND TURNED INTO FELT TO MAKE HATS.

CANADA'S BEAVERS WERE HAPPY WHEN FELT HATS WENT OUT OF FASHION.

SASKATCHEWAN
Land of Living Skies

Western Red Lily

Sharptailed Grouse

Regina

Here we are in Saskatchewan! This province wins the prize for having the straightest borders on the map. But it loses points because it's hard to spell.

Regina

Yesterday we arrived in the capital city, Regina. We went to Wascana Lake. A hundred years ago, there was no lake in Regina, so they made one. Smart thinking. Next they should build a mountain. It's quite flat here.

This is RCMP country (Royal Canadian Mounted Police). There's a training center for new police officers here. If Gran doesn't behave, we'll call the cops!

Wheat fields

Moose Jaw

Things you should know about Moose Jaw.

1. It has dozens of murals painted on buildings.

2. It also has a jet training base. That's where the Snowbird jet pilots learn to do aerial tricks. Earplugs recommended.

3. Moose Jaw has underground tunnels. A hundred years ago, Chinese workers washed clothes for thirty-five cents a day in the hot, steamy laundry down there. They even slept underground. They were trying to earn enough money so their families in China could afford to move to Canada to join them. We walked through the tunnels and it was like walking back in time. Actors dressed in costumes showed us what a hard life it was!

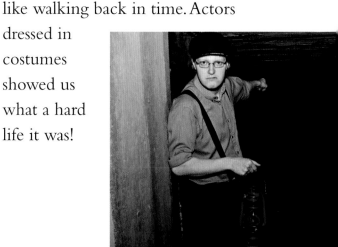

🔍 FIND IT!

- Wheatfield
- Bison
- Grain elevator
- RCMP

Natural Prairie Grasslands

We drove around most of the day trying to find bison in Grasslands National Park. You'd think it would be hard to hide a herd of bison! We finally spied them, and watched for a while through the binocs. From the car. Bison are big! And Fact Dispenser read

that they are "unpredictable."

The park looks like the prairies did before people started farming. Long ago, huge herds of bison (also known as buffalo) used to roam the prairies. Then hunters with guns arrived, and soon the bison were almost gone. At the park, they are trying to turn that around. The herd is getting bigger every year.

Woof

Populations of prairie dogs nearly disappeared out on the prairies too, and the Parks people are helping to increase their numbers. Ranchers used to shoot them because they dug holes in the fields.

Prairie dogs are really squirrels, not dogs. They stand at the entrance to their burrows and pretend not to be looking at you. Sometimes they throw back their heads and bark out a warning "yip!"

"We're reintroducing the black-footed ferrets too," said the Parks guide. She said these animals had disappeared from the wild and were only alive in zoos. Now some of them live in the park.

"Do they get along with the prairie dogs?" Cal asked.

"Ferrets eat them," she said. "But we have enough prairie dogs that we can afford to lose some to the ferrets."

"Do the prairie dogs know about this plan?" asked Gran.

Cypress Hills

Cypress Hills is the highest bump in Saskatchewan. From the top, you can look out over a sea of prairie. During the ice ages long ago, these hills stuck up above the ice that covered the rest of the prairies.

Our campsite is in trees, for a change. Usually the prairies are too dry for trees. There's a problem with trees, though. The squirrels up there keep bombing our tent with pinecones.

Here's an old wooden grain elevator beside the railroad tracks. The grain is stored in the top and slides down a chute into the railway boxcars to be transported to other places.

Fort Walsh

Fort Walsh was a North-West Mounted Police fort. In 1875, the red-coated Mounties came riding onto the prairies.

They brought law and order. Good thing, too, because people were stealing horses and shooting each other. (The NWMP later became the RCMP.)

We made round pillbox hats like the NWMP used to wear. Then we put them on and did our marching drill. We arrested Gran and took her to the jail. She demanded we let her out.

"What if we don't?" I asked.

"I'll sing!"

"You're free to go!" said Cal quickly.

IT'S THE TRUTH! (Cal's Factoid)

Towns formed along the railway. Sometimes they were given names in alphabetical order. Some of those places have now disappeared. But on the map, we found Fenwood, Goodeve, Hubbard, Ituna, Jasmine, Kelliher, and LeRoss – all in a row.

ALBERTA
Cowboys & Dinosaurs

White Trillium

Edmonton

Great Horned
Owl

Dinosaurs roam in southern Alberta! That's not quite true. They *used* to roam here, seventy-five million years ago. Today all that's left are dinosaur fossils.

GRAN WROTE A POEM

A dino came out to play
At Dinosaur Park today.
A mighty Gorgosaurus
Appeared before us.
Cal said, "Good gracious!
"Escaped from the Late Cretacious!"
Alice patted it on the head.
"I thought you all were all dead.
"I'm glad you're here instead.
"Mind if I call you Fred?"

FRED

FIND IT!

• Dinosaur
• Hoodoo
• Oil pump
• Snow

At Dinosaur Provincial Park, we went on a dig for fossils. Our tour bus drove into the dusty badlands. We found old pieces of bone, but our guide wasn't very excited. She said they came from something a lot smaller than a dinosaur.

The big dinosaur fossils were at the Royal Tyrrell Museum in Drumheller. Huge skeletons. Truly terrifying! Fact Dispenser knew all of their names, of course. Hello, stegosaurus. Pleased to meet you, tyrannosaurus rex. Cal also learned some new dino names – like albertosaurus and mojoceratops!

"They should name the next dinosaur they find aliceosaurus," Cal said.

"Aliceosaurus! A truly awesome dinosaur," said Gran.

"Roar!" I said, baring my teeth and clawing with my hands.

Here's a hoodoo! Water has worn the rock into crazy mushroom shapes.

Hoodoo ↘

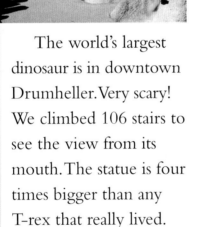

The world's largest dinosaur is in downtown Drumheller. Very scary! We climbed 106 stairs to see the view from its mouth. The statue is four times bigger than any T-rex that really lived.

Hay fields on the w-i-d-e prairies! The wind blows a lot, which is bad for my hair but good for windmills making wind power. Can you see the Rocky Mountains in the distance! We're headed that-a-way!

Hay fields

Calgary

Howdy! We're in cowboy country, even though we're in a big city. Calgary is known as Cowtown. The Calgary Stampede happens here every summer. Giddyup!

We went to Canada Olympic Park. It was built for the 1988 Calgary Winter Olympics. You can do lots of sports that get your heart thumping. We watched people ride a zipline from the top of the ski jump. It zips at 140 kilometers (87 miles) per hour.

"Too scary!" Cal said.

"Too expensive!" Gran said.

Edmonton

From Calgary, we drove north to Edmonton. The two Alberta cities are rivals.

"Calgary is bigger," said Cal.

"But Edmonton is the capital city," I said. "Right, Gran?"

"I'm staying out of it," said Gran.

We took a riverboat ride along the North Saskatchewan River. It goes right through Edmonton, so it's a good way to visit the city. We saw the fancy parliament buildings where the government meets. Cal ducked when we went under the bridges.

Then we visited Fort Edmonton, a fur trading post. A lot of prairie cities, like Calgary and Edmonton, started out as trading posts. People living back

then would sure be surprised to see the skyscrapers in those cities today!

We are trying to persuade Gran to take us to the West Edmonton Mall.

"It's the world's biggest shopping mall!" I said.

"I hate shopping malls," said Gran.

"But this one has a pirate ship. The world's largest waterslides! Mini-ature golf! A fake reef with real seals

swimming around!" I said.

"And escalators," said Cal.

We'll keep working on her.

Strange sighting. This pump-jack goes up and down, up and down. It is pumping out oil from under the ground. Alberta has lots of hidden oil.

The Rocky Mountains

We drove up to the Rocky Mountains. Good-bye, flat prairies! Some mountains still had snow on them, even though it's summer.

We stopped at the Athabasca Glacier. That's where drivers in snowcoaches with huge tires take tourists for tours on the ice.

But not us. We went on an ice walk with a mountain guide. We put on hiking boots, warm clothes, and even tuques. Our guide Peter gave us spiky

crampons to strap on to our boots. That way, we could walk on the ice and not slip. He said we were walking on the tongue of the glacier.

"Does it have ears too?" Cal asked.

"Ignore him," Gran said to Peter. "He's been cooped up in the car for too long."

Peter let us look into a crevasse, a big crack in the ice. The ice inside was blue. He explained that the glacier is made of snow that doesn't melt, and instead gets squished into ice. But the climate is getting warmer, so now the glaciers are melting. Some day they may melt away completely.

Peter found a safe place where we could slide on our bums down some snow. Now I have a wet bum. It was worth it.

IT'S THE TRUTH! (Cal's Factoid)

During the ice ages, long ago, glaciers covered most of Canada. Cities like Edmonton were buried under ice.

Banff

Afterward, we drove down the highway to Banff. There was a traffic jam because drivers stopped to look at mountain sheep grazing on the side of the road.

In Banff, we made a beeline for the hot springs pool. From ice to steaming-hot swimming in one day! Later we took a gondola up the mountain. At the top, we were 2,281 meters (7,486 feet) above sea level. That's the highest I've ever been in my whole life, except on an airplane. And every direction I looked, I saw more mountains. This is one scrunched-up landscape!

AT THE BUFFALO JUMP

1000 YEARS AGO. BISON THUNDERED ACROSS THE PRAIRIES.

THE PLAINS INDIANS LIVED THEIR LIVES AROUND THE BUFFALO. THE ANIMALS PROVIDED THEM WITH MEAT, TEPEE COVERINGS, CLOTHING...ALMOST EVERYTHING THEY NEEDED.

THIS BAG—IS IT REALLY MADE FROM A BUFFALO BLADDER? WOW!

WHERE DID YOU FIND FIREWOOD? THERE ARE NO TREES!

I'M BURNING DRIED BUFFALO DUNG.

HUNTING BUFFALO BEFORE THERE WERE GUNS...

KEEP 'EM MOVING TOWARD THE BUFFALO JUMP!

THE BISONS WERE QUICKLY CUT UP FOR USE.

THIS JUMP WAS USED FOR OVER 5000 YEARS! CLOSE YOUR EYES AND IMAGINE THE GROUND SHAKING.

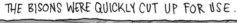

Pacific Dogwood

BRITISH COLUMBIA
To the Pacific!

Victoria

Steller's Jay

We're still in the Rockies but we've just crossed the border into British Columbia (which I'll call BC). Our last province!

"From here, it's downhill to the Pacific Ocean, right?" I asked.

"Um . . . not quite. Lots of ups and downs along the way," said Gran.

No kidding. It turns out that BC is mostly mountains.

Squeezing Through the Mountains

At Rogers Pass, the Trans-Canada Highway squishes through a gap in the wall of mountains. In winter, snow avalanches come crashing down the steep slopes. The road goes through snow sheds for protection. The snow slides right over the top. The train avoids avalanches by going through a tunnel in the mountain.

We stopped where the last spike was banged into the Canadian Pacific Railway line in 1885. The railway across Canada was built from opposite ends, and it joined here. Here's a famous photo of important people wearing top hats, banging in the spike.

"Canada from sea to sea," said Gran, reading the sign. "That's a very long way."

"We oughta know!" said Cal.

Searching for Ogopogo

We took a detour to Okanagan Lake for more beach time – Cal floating on his polka-dotted dragon, me trying to stay upright on my killer whale. Gran sits under a beach umbrella, eating cherries that turn her teeth purple. We've been buying peaches, cherries, and apricots from the fruit stands that line the highways. It's too hot to cook anyhow.

An Ogopogo lives in Okanagan Lake . . . so they say. Few have actually seen this mysterious monster. Does the Ogopogo really exist? Or is it phony?

I'll tell you when I see it.

 **FIND IT!**

- Totem pole
- Mountain
- Ogopogo
- SkyTrain
- Sea star
- Pacific Ocean (just a taste)

Hamster Update

Houdini is captured! Last night I decided to sleep in the car. In the pitch-dark, I heard a little noise. Then something tickled my face! I shrieked and Gran came running from the tent. When she opened the car door and the light came on, there was Houdini on the front seat, cheeks bulging with food. Gran is buying a steel cage today.

Follow the Fraser

Back on the Trans-Canada Highway, we're following the Fraser River south to Vancouver. The river runs through a deep canyon. The road clings to the canyon walls. Gran is holding tight to the steering wheel. From his seat, Cal can see down – way down – to the river below.

We stopped at Hell's Gate Rapids. You can look down on the churning water from a suspension bridge. Once a cow called Rosie accidentally floated through the rapids, and lived to moo about it.

Vancouver

Hello, Pacific Ocean. Bet you thought we'd never get here! (You aren't the only one.)

Vancouver is surrounded by sea and mountains. We took a gondola up a mountain to see the view. From the top, we looked down on Vancouver's skyscrapers. We watched a freighter come into the harbor.

We could also see a big green area – Stanley Park. Later we went in-line skating on the seawall path around the park. We stopped by some tall totem poles carved by aboriginal British Columbians. Before this area was Stanley Park, there were First Nations villages here. I learned that each figure on the pole – like a raven or a frog – is called a totem. Sometimes the totems tell a family's story. Instead of writing the story in a book, it's carved into a totem pole.

We ate lunch on a sandy beach in the park. The sand blew into my sandwich.

"That's why they are called sand-wiches," Gran said.

"I can't hear you," I said.

There was less sand at the Vancouver Aquarium. And the baby sea otters were adorable. Did you know a sea otter can float on its back and use its tummy as a table?

Here is Vancouver's Sky-Train. It has no drivers. An onboard computer communicates back and forth with the control center.

Whistler

We drove to Whistler. It's where the 2010 Winter Olympics were held. We took a ride on a gondola that hangs from a long cable stretching between two mountains. Gran's knees got wobbly looking down to the valley floor more than four hundred meters (1,312 feet) below.

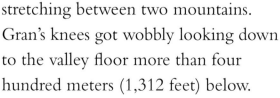

Victoria

A big ferry took us to Vancouver Island. We put our hands over our ears when the ship's horn blew. Greedy seagulls chased us across the ocean, hoping for handouts.

You'd think Vancouver would be on Vancouver Island. But no, it's on the mainland. Instead, the biggest city on Vancouver Island is Victoria. It's the capital of BC.

Victoria pretends to be very English. Maybe because the city was named after a queen of England. You can even ride an English double-decker bus.

"We should 'ave a cuppa tea," I said, trying to sound properly English.

"I don't like tea," said Cal. "And you sound silly."

"Follow me," said Gran. "I know a very English-y thing to do!" Down at the harbor, we boarded a tiny ferryboat. It scooted across the water, dodging sailboats and incoming seaplanes. We got off at a dock where you could buy English-style fish and chips.

"Jolly good!" I said, still working on my English accent.

"Gran, make her stop," said Cal.

"Let's go feed her to the mammoth," said Gran.

At the Museum

A life-size mammoth lives in the Royal BC Museum. It looked fierce, but I wasn't fooled. I knew mammoths were extinct. They only lived long ago, during the ice ages. Grizzly bears are not extinct, so

that's more scary. But the ones at the museum were stuffed. Did you know that one-quarter of the world's grizzly bears lives in BC?

"Should I worry about grizzly attacks?" I asked.

"If you like," Gran said. "But I wouldn't bother."

Gran and I wandered into the

history part of the museum to see Captain George Vancouver's ship arriving on the coast in the 1790s. I blame him for all those confusing Vancouver names.

"Where's Cal?" Gran suddenly asked.

We found him riding the escalator.

Here's the beginning of the Trans-Canada Highway to St. John's, Newfoundland. We did it all – 7,604 kilometers (4,725 miles) – but I guess we did it backward!

Long Beach. Exceedingly Long.

At Long Beach, we're about as far west as we can be in southern Canada. The sand beaches stretch on for miles. The wind blows. The breakers crash. The water is cold! Surfers in wet suits play on the waves. This is the Pacific Ocean. Nothing but sea and sky, all the way to . . .

"Japan," said Gran.

"Are we going to Japan?" asked Cal.

"No way," said Gran. "We're not done with Canada yet. The North calls!"

IT'S THE TRUTH! (Cal's Factoid)

If a starfish's arm gets ripped off, another arm will grow in its place. Bonus fact: scientists say that a starfish is not really a fish, so they would like you to call it a sea star instead.

North to the Yukon

From Vancouver Island, we took an overnight ferry ride up the coast to Prince Rupert. Then, back to driving. First to the town of Dawson Creek. It's at Mile 0 on the Alaska Highway going north. Then, onward to the Yukon! (We'll stop before we get to Alaska, which is part of the United States.)

At Liard River Hot Springs, we stopped for a warm soak, and that washed off our bug spray. On our walk back to the campsite, we were eaten alive by mosquitoes. But we also saw a moose!

BUILDING THE CANADIAN PACIFIC RAILWAY

YUKON
Going North!

Fireweed

Raven

Whitehorse

Hi, Yukon!

We've come to find gold! We've been learning about the Klondike gold rush. In 1898, the word got out — "Thar's gold in the Yukon!" And the stampede began! Some people didn't even know where the Yukon was — they just followed the other people rushing for gold.

"Maybe there's some gold left," I said. "I could strike it rich!"

"A sucker born every minute," said Gran.

Before we go find the gold, we need to check out Whitehorse, Yukon's capital city.

Exploring Whitehorse

The SS *Klondike* is a stern-wheeler that used to take miners up the Yukon River to the goldfields. A stern-wheeler has a big wheel at the back (the stern). When the wheel spins, the blades pull the boat through the water. This one doesn't go anywhere these days. It's turned into a museum.

Watson Lake Signpost Forest along the Alaska Highway. The forest started with one sign in 1942. Now there are over sixty thousand

FIND IT!

- Stern-wheeler
- Yukon River
- Sabre-toothed tiger
- Gold dredge
- Gold!

We went inside a log church that's over one hundred years old. There we learned about a bishop who ate his boots. He got lost for fifty-one days in the Yukon wilderness, and he ran out of food. So he boiled and toasted pieces of some boots he was carrying. They were made of sealskin and walrus skin so that helped to keep him alive.

"These days people would use a cell phone and call for rescue," said Cal.

"Or call for pizza," said Gran.

Miles Canyon

Those crazy gold rushers! After hiking over the mountains into the Yukon, they piled their stuff onto boats or rafts for the trip down the Yukon River to the gold. Some boats flipped over in the rapids. One place where that happened a lot was right here – Miles Canyon, near Whitehorse.

"They say the waves looked like *white horses* tossing their manes," Gran said as we stood on the footbridge looking down into the water.

Not anymore. A dam on the river has made the water flat.

"Let me try that again," said Gran. "The waves looked like *white horses*. Get it?"

Aha! That's where Whitehorse got its name!

Beringia

Strange beasts were sighted at the Yukon Beringia Interpretive Centre. These gigantic animals lived up north during

the ice ages, along with the mammoths. One was a giant beaver the size of a black bear. Another was a fierce cat the size of a lion. This saber-toothed tiger had long, sharp teeth.

The museum guide taught us how to shoot an atlatl. It was a weapon used by hunters to take down mammoths. Our practice mammoth was made of plywood. I missed it by a long shot.

"You'll be no help when we are attacked by a mammoth," said Gran. "How will you defend us?"

"I'll stick out my tongue," I said.

Along the Klondike Highway

We're not floating down the Yukon River to Dawson City like those crazy gold rushers. We're driving there along the Klondike Highway.

Lake Laberge along the Klondike Hwy

First stop: Cinnamon Bun Strip. It's famous for cinnamon buns.

"Buy three," I said.

Gran bought just one – the biggest cinnamon bun I ever saw. We commenced a three-way attack. The bun was soon demolished.

FIVE FINGER RAPIDS

We stopped and walked down to the river to see some rapids. Four islands divide the river into five channels (the five fingers). Floating downstream, the gold seekers had to be sure to pick the right channel. Going up the river was even harder. The steamboats had to be pulled against the current with a cable and a winch.

Dawson City

Dawson City still looks a lot like it did in the gold rush days. The tourists like it that way. We found Robert Service's cabin. He wrote poems like "The Cremation of Sam McGee." You should read that one. An actor in Dawson City now pretends to be Robert Service and reads his stories to tourists.

We also found where Pierre Berton, another Yukon author, lived.

"He wrote *The Secret World of Og*," said Gran. "Remember that book?"

"Og," said Cal.

Thar's Gold!

Of course, we tried panning for gold. We scooped sand from the river bottom into our pan. Swirled it around. Sloshed off the top stuff. And looked for the gold nuggets that sink to the bottom.

I struck gold! My chunk is about the size of a grain of sand. Gran needed to put on her reading glasses to see it. I'm rich.

Dredge #4

After the goldpanners were finished, big dredges like this one moved into the creeks. The dredges scooped up gravel, removing any remaining gold. You can still see the big piles of dirt they left behind. This dredge was the biggest – eight storeys high.

The Dempster Highway

Warning: 720 kilometers (447 miles) of gravel road ahead! Gran wants to drive the Dempster Highway to Inuvik (how to say it: "In-oo-vik"). It's in the North-west Territories. We'll do the drive in three days, camping along the way. There aren't many gas stations. We're carrying an extra spare tire and extra gas in a plastic container.

When I next report in, we'll be above the Arctic Circle!

NORTHWEST TERRITORIES
Land of the Midnight Sun!

Gyrfalcon

Yellowknife

Mountain Avens

Inuvik

"I thought there would be snow and ice everywhere," I said.

"That's called winter," said Gran. "And this is summer."

This far north, the sun shines almost all night. It never gets dark. It's hard to get to sleep in our tent. Cal is getting cranky.

"Am not!" he says in a cranky voice.

The Inuit people who live in this part of the Northwest Territories (NWT) are called Inuvialuit. The First Nations people are Gwich'in. People live in houses that are painted purple, turquoise, and other bright colors. It's very cheery. Many buildings are off the ground, built on stilts. That's because

the ground is frozen under the top layer, but this top layer can melt a bit in summer, and houses sitting on the ground can tilt. Trees lean over too, because they can't push their roots deep into the frozen ground.

The afternoon was spent at the swimming pool, playing on the waterslide. Meanwhile, Gran got our flat tires fixed.

We are above the Arctic Circle. We even got a certificate from the tourism office to prove it!

Bear witness that

Alice and Calvin

having demonstrated the initiative, integrity, and bold adventurous spirit of the true Arctic explorers who have crossed the Arctic Circle will hereafter be recognized as an honorable member of the exclusive Polar Bear Chapter, Order of Arctic Adventurers.

The Mackenzie River

From our campsite, we can see the Mackenzie River – the longest river in Canada. It flows over four thousand kilometers (2,485 miles) through NWT. By the time it gets to Inuvik, it is near the end of its journey to the Arctic Ocean. It spreads out into a tangle of channels, lakes, and sandbars, still flowing north. Gran calls this the delta.

We are saying good-bye to the car! Some friends will drive it home for us. We're flying back across the Arctic Circle to Yellowknife.

"Houdini's coming on the plane with us, right?" asked Cal.

Gran sighed. "What will the pilot say? But we can't leave him here! He'd run away and join the lemmings."

Ferry crossing Mackenzie River

FIND IT!

- House on stilts
- Musk ox
- Mackenzie River
- Mosquitoes
- Colorful houses

Yellowknife

We're here, in the Diamond Capital of North America (because there are diamond mines nearby). This is also NWT's capital. And Gran says we're in Denendeh – the land of the Dene people.

"Did they live here long ago?" I asked.

"They live here now," said Gran. "Check out their Facebook page."

We started our Yellowknife visit at the top of a hill called The Rock. We looked down on the old part of Yellowknife that sticks out into Great Slave Lake. You can watch floatplanes taking off from the lake. They take people into the wilderness. There is no end of lakes out there to land on.

The Wildcat Café was nearby. It's a very old log cabin that was once almost torn down. But the people in Whitehorse saved it, and now it's a famous landmark. Gran said maybe we should go there for supper.

"What kind of food?" asked Cal.

"Oh, caribou, musk ox . . . stuff like that," said Gran.

"I'm allergic," said Cal.

Then off to Frame Lake. We walked around the lake until the mosquitoes had sucked all our blood. Then we went inside the Prince of Wales Museum to check out some NWT animals. We found caribou, polar bears, musk ox, and lots more. The thing about animals

that live in museums is that you can get close up without being eaten or trampled. Also, there are no bugs.

Outside Yellowknife

We rented a car to explore some lakes you can drive to from Yellowknife. Gran said she wanted to leave at dawn so we could see lots of wildlife.

"But dawn is at, like, two o'clock," said Cal. "It hardly ever gets dark up here."

Good point. We left later, after some noisy ravens woke us up. On our drive, we saw a black bear and a fox. Cal said he saw a lynx when we weren't looking.

"I very much doubt that," said Gran.

We visited the Cameron River waterfall (the sign warned visitors not

to fall down the cliff, so we didn't). Then we camped beside a good lake for swimming. We are becoming Arctic beach bums. Gran was happy because she could watch loons out on the lake.

Tomorrow we leave NWT. On to Nunavut, our last territory in Canada! We're taking another plane. All this flying costs a lot. But there's no other way to get there. And we can't miss

out on Nunavut!

"We'll pay you back when we're grown up and rich," I said.

"I'll write that down so I don't forget," said Gran.

SEARCHING FOR THE NORTHWEST PASSAGE

Purple Saxifrage

nunAvuT
"Our Land"

Rock Ptarmigan

We're in Iqaluit. It's Canada's smallest capital city. It's on Canada's biggest island, Baffin Island. How big is Baffin? Gran figured out that Prince Edward Island would fit into Baffin Island about ninety times.

Most people who live in Nunavut are Inuit. Kids in school learn both English and Inuktitut, which is the Inuit language. Here's your Inuktitut lesson for today: "Iqaluit" means "place of many fish." "Inuit" means "the people." And according to Cal, who has the guidebook, "kaakpunga" means "I am hungry." That one could come in handy.

Exploring Iqaluit

There are no trees here. It's wide open, with rocky, rolling hills and tundra, and views over the ocean. The wind blows!

Lots of women wear a parka called an amounti (how to say it: "a-moun-tee"). On the back, there's a pouch for carrying a baby and keeping it snug. People ride around on ATVs – all-terrain vehicles. In winter they use snowmobiles. Some people still have dog teams, but usually just for fun. You can see the dogs chained up outside their houses.

Some things here are modern – like cell phones and ATMs. Some are the same as they've been for hundreds of years, like going caribou hunting.

Inuit Games

At the visitor center, we tried some Inuit games. I am going to have to practice! One was the One-Foot High Kick. Imagine a ball hanging from a string, about my height off the ground. Run up to it, jump off from both feet, kick high to hit the ball with one foot, then land on that same foot and keep your balance.

Here's another game, called Kneel Jump. You kneel on the ground. Swing your arms back to get ready. Then, all at once, swing your arms forward, lift your body into the air, and land on your feet. You should land as far forward as you can. Try not to fall on your nose.

FIND IT!

- Inukshuk
- Arctic cotton
- Dog team
- Throat singing

Throat Singing

We watched some Inuit drum dancing and throat singing. It's not like any singing I've ever heard before. Two singers face each other and make strange twanging, buzzing, humming sounds to the same beat, using their breath and their voices. Gran and I tried it until I got the giggles.

At the waterfront, we watched some freighters coming in. They bring food that won't grow here in the north.

Cal found a place where he could dip his toe in the ocean.

"Is this really the Arctic Ocean?" he asked.

"Close enough," said Gran. "We're in the Arctic. It's ocean."

Outside Iqaluit

For our last day, we went hiking and had a picnic at a park outside of town. Gran is now in a very good mood

because she saw a gyrfalcon! It's the biggest, fastest, strongest falcon in the world. It can scare the heck out of the ptarmigan it hunts. We also kept eyes peeled for the ptarmigan. The birds are hard to see. In summer, they turn the same color as the rocks. If a gyrfalcon was after me, I'd probably try to blend in too.

Arctic birds build their nests on the ground. "Guess why?" asked Gran.

"How about . . . because there's no trees!" Cal said.

He was right (as usual). No trees on the tundra. At first it looks all barren and rocky. But when you look closer, there are lots of flowers near the ground. Even some blueberries to gobble. Gran pointed out the arctic cotton. The Inuit used it for a wick in their stone lamps. They burned seal blubber or caribou fat.

Inukshuk

An inukshuk! The name means "that which stands for a man." These stone figures helped the Inuit find their way across the tundra. In a blizzard, it's easy to get lost, but the inukshuk showed the route. They were used for other purposes too, such as to mark the best place to launch a kayak.

Good-bye to the North

We went out for a good-bye dinner on our last night in Nunavut. Gran ordered arctic char (it tasted like salmon). I had a musk ox burger slathered in relish. Cal even took a bite – amazing! Gran said it was too bad there was no maktaaq on the menu – raw whale skin and blubber.

"That's OK," said Cal.

Tomorrow we're flying to Ottawa. My parents probably won't recognize me. I'm taller. Smarter. I am, after all, an expert on Canada.

TRIP'S END

"Wow, we did it!" said Gran while we waited at the Iqaluit airport. "Coast to coast to coast. Every province and territory. Every capital city. What grandchildren I have. What troopers! How do you feel?"

"Really grubby," I said. "When did I last have a proper bath?"

"The trip was good, but next time let's find a smaller country," said Cal. "Canada was kind of big."

"Next time?" said Gran.

"One part of me is really looking forward to going home," I said. "But one part of me is not."

Gran nodded. "I know the feeling. But thank you both for sharing this trip with me. It just wouldn't have been the same without you."

"And Houdini," I reminded her.

"He definitely added to the trip," Gran agreed.

"Uh-oh," said Cal. Gran and I quickly looked at him. He was patting his pockets, looking worried. The hamster cage was empty. "Where . . . ?"

CAL'S TWEET

Hamster is happy he's going home to sleep in his own bed. Bye-bye, Canada!

Gran looked up at the ceiling. "No, not again!"

"Here he is!" Cal grinned and pulled Houdini out from his sleeve. "I was looking in the wrong place."

Gran gave him her most ferocious glare.

"Say, Gran?" I asked.

"Yes?"

"Is it OK if I ask you something?"

"Of course, Alice," she said.

"So, um . . . , " I looked at Cal. He nodded and we both asked, "Are we there yet?"

Gran took a huge breath and held it. We covered our ears. Surely she wouldn't sing opera loudly in the middle of the Iqaluit airport? Then she let her breath out, and grinned. "You bet we are! Let's go home, travelers!"

It all began in Newfoundland

As we set out to visit this supersized land!

There were oceans and mountains, tundra and prairie,

A moose on the loose and a T-Rex most scary.

Cal fed us the facts and kept Alice from snoring,

I don't snore!

The hamster made sure the trip never got boring.

But our journey is done, and we're all headed home,

So this, fellow travelers, is your final poem

. . . until next time!

THE BIG PICTURE:
This Land of Ours

FLAGS OF CANADA

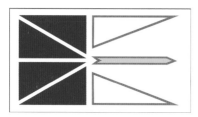
Newfoundland

Quebec

British Columbia

Nova Scotia

Ontario

Yukon

Prince Edward Island

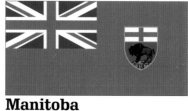
Manitoba

Northwest Territories

Saskatchewan

New Brunswick

Alberta

Nunavut

PHOTOGRAPHY CREDITS

All photos ©Vivien Bowers, except: 8 Signal Hill © Parks Canada; 8-9 cod © iStockphoto.com/OKRAD; 9 St. John's colorful houses © iStockphoto.com/Chiyacat; 10 puffin © iStockphoto.com/plinney; 11 Cabot Trail © Parks Canada; 12 guillemot © iStockphoto.com/Ivkovich; 12 changing of the guard, Citadel © novascotia.com; 13 Halifax waterfront © novascotia.com; 13 scallops © iStockphoto.com/tladams; 14 haggis © iStockphoto.com/PaulCowan; 16 Founders' Hall ©Tourism Charlottetown and Founders' Hall Museum; 17 Green Gables © Parks Canada; 17 Confederation bridge © 1970 steve/Dreamstime.com; 18 low tide © iStockphoto.com/SimplyCreativePhotography; 20 Acadian village © Village Historique Acadien; 21 French road signs © iStockphoto.com/bigstevemac; 22-23 Château Frontenac © Fairmont Le Château Frontenac; 24 Montreal skyline © iStockphoto.com/AK2; 23 Old Montreal © iStockphoto.com/DenisTangneyJr; 24 Montreal and Big O © iStockphoto.com/buzbuzzer; 26 grotesque, Parliament building © National Capital Commission; 27 Centennial flame © iStockphoto.com/buzbuzzer; 28 Famous Five statue © National Capital Commission; 28 CN Tower © Km2008/Dreamstime.com; 31 porcupine © Science North & Dynamic Earth; 31 Big Nickel © Sudbury Tourism; 32 Wawa goose statue © James Smedley; 32 Terry Fox statue © Tourism & Economic Development, City of Thunder Bay; 35 yellow-headed blackbird © iStockphoto.com/lightstalker; 38 RCMP officer © (2010) HER MAJESTY THE QUEEN IN RIGHT OF CANADA as represented by the Royal Canadian Mounted Police (RCMP), reprinted with permission of the RCMP; 38 tunnels of Moose Jaw ©Tunnels of Moose Jaw; 39 bison © Parks Canada; 40 Fort Walsh © Parks Canada; 42 hoodoo © iStockphoto.com/jewhyte; 43 Edmonton and river boat ride © iStockphoto.com/InStock; 43 West Edmonton Mall © West Edmonton Mall; 43 pump-jack © iStockphoto.com/ImagineGolf; 43 Athabasca Glacier © Parks Canada; 44 view from Sulphur Mountain at the top of the Banff gondola © iStockphoto.com/phototerry; 46 Rogers Pass © Eric White; 46 Last Spike on the CPR archival photograph © Library and Archives Canada; 48 Stanley Park seawall © iStockphoto.com/dan_prat; 48 totem pole © iStockphoto.com/Gregory Olsen; 48 sea otter © iStockphoto.com/ErnestBielfeldt; 48 Vancouver SkyTrain © iStockphoto.com/AnthonyRosenberg; 48 Whistler gondola © iStockphoto.com/candatsystems; 49 BC Ferry © Eric White; 49 double-decker bus © Eric White; 49 mammoth at Royal BC Museum © Woolly Mammoth, Royal BC Museum, Victoria; 50 Mile 0 of the Trans-Canada Highway © Eric White; 50 Liard River Hot Springs © iStockphoto.com/audreynolte-painter; 52 Watson Lake signpost forest © iStockphoto.com/Lisay; 54 scimitar cat © Beringia Interpretive Centre; 54 Five Finger Rapids © iStockphoto.com/eppicphotography; 55 Dredge #4 © Parks Canada; 56 colorful houses in Inuvik © Government of the Northwest Territories; 57 ferry across the Mackenzie River at Tsiigehtchic on the Dempster Highway © Government of the Northwest Territories; 58 aerial view of Yellowknife © iStockphoto.com/RyersonClark; 61 Inuit children © Nunavut Tourism; 63 gyrfalcon © iStockphoto.com/M-Reinhardt; 63 inukshuk © Robcocquyt/Dreamstime.com.

INDEX

A

Acadia, **20**
Acadian Village, 20
Alaska highway, 52
Alberta, **41-44**
Anne of Green Gables. *See* Green Gables
Arctic Circle, 56
arctic cotton, 63
Assiniboine River, 33
Athabasca Glacier, 43-44

B

Baffin Island, 61
bagels, 23
baguette, 22
Baie Saint-Paul, 22
Banff, **44**
Bay of Fundy, **18**
bears, grizzly, 49
beavers, 31, 35, 37
Beringia Interpretive Centre, **53-54**
Berton, Pierre, 55
Big Nickel, **31**
Big O Olympic Games stadium, 24
Biodome, **24**
bison, 39, 45
black-footed ferret, 39
boulangerie, 22
Britain, 8, 12, 14, 15, 19, 25
British Columbia, **46-50**
buffalo jump, **45**

C

cable ferries, 19
Cabot Trail, 11-12
Calgary, **42**
Calgary Stampede, 42
Cameron River waterfall, 59
Canada, founding, 16
Canada, physical map, 66-67
Canada, political map, 6-7
Canada Olympic Park, 42
Canadian Pacific Railway, 46, **51**
Canadian Shield, **32**
Cape Breton Island, 11
Cape Spear, 8
caribou, 10, 58, 62
ceilidh, 11
Centennial flame, **27**
Champlain, Samuel de, 13-14
Charlevoix, 22
Charlottetown, **16**

Château Frontenac, 23
Chinese launderers, 38
Cinnamon Bun Strip, 54
Citadel, 12
CN Tower, **28**
coal mine, 12
cod, 9
Confederation, Fathers and Ladies of, 16
Confederation Bridge, **17**
covered bridges, 18
Cree, 33
Cypress Hills, **40**

D

Dawson City, **55**
Dempster Highway, **55**
Denendeh, 58
Digby, **13**
Dinosaur Provincial Park, 41
dog teams, 61
dredges, **55**
Drumheller, 41, 42
dulse, 20

E

Edmonton, **42-43**

F

Famous Five statue, 28
First Nations, 35, 48, 56-57
Five Finger Rapids, **54**
fleur-de-lis, 23
Forks, the, **33-34**
Fort Edmonton, 43
Fort Walsh, **40**
Fortress Louisbourg, **15**
Founders' Hall, 16
Frame Lake, 58
France, 8, 12, 14, 15, 25
Franklin, Sir John, 60
Fraser River, 47
Fredericton, **19**
French, as language, 20, 23, 33
fur trade, 35, **37**

G

gannets, 21
Garrison District, 19
Gaspé Peninsula, **21**
Georgian Bay, **30-31**
glacier, 43-44
gold, 52-53, 55

Golden Boy, 33-34
gondola, Whistler, 48
grain elevator, 40
Grasslands National Park, **39**
Great Lakes, **29, 30**
Great Slave Lake, 58
Green Gables, **17**
guillemots, 12
Gulf of Saint Lawrence, 21
Gwich'in, 56-57
gyrfalcon, 63

H
haggis, 14
Halifax, **12-13**
Halifax Harbour, **13**
hay fields, 42
Hell's Gate Rapids, 47
hoodoo, 42
Hopewell Cape, 18
Hudson Bay Company, 35

I
iceberg, **9**
Île Bonaventure, 21
Inuit, 56, 61,62, 63
Inuit games, 52, **62**
inukshuk, **63**
Inuktitut, 61
Inuvialuit, 56
Inuvik, **56**
Iqaluit, 61
Iroquoian village, Hochelega, 24

J
joie de vivre, 24

K
Kensington Market, 29
Kings Landing, 19
Klondike gold rush. *See* gold
Klondike Highway, **54**
Kneel Jump, 62
Kouchibouguac national park, **20**

L
L'Anse aux Meadows, **10**
Lake Ontario, 28
Lake Superior, **31**
Liard River Hot Springs, 50
lobster pot, 14
locks (water system), 30
Long Beach, **50**
Lower Fort Garry, **35**

M
Mackenzie River, **57**
mammoth, 49, 54
Manitoba, **33-36**
Miles Canyon, **53**
Mont Royal, **23**
Montreal, **23-24**
moose, **10**
Moose Jaw, **38**
Museum of Civilization, 27
musk ox, 58

N
Narrows, the, 8
National War Memorial, 28
New Brunswick, **18-20**
Newfoundland and Labrador, **8-10**
Niagara Escarpment, **30**
Niagara Falls, **29**
Norsemen, 10
North Saskatchewan River, 42-43
North-West Mounted Police (NWMP), 40
Northwest Passage, **60**
Northwest Territories, **56-59**
Nova Scotia, **11-14**
Nunavut, **61-63**

O
Ogopogo, **47**
oil, 43
Okanagan Lake, 47
Old Montreal. *See* Montreal
One-Foot High Kick, 62
Ontario, **26-32**
Ottawa, **26-28**

P
Pacific Ocean, 48, 50
Parliament buildings, **26-27**
pemmican, 37
Pierced Rock. *See* Rocher Percé
pitcher plant, **10**
Plains Indians, 45
Plains of Abraham, **25**
porcupine, 31
Port-Royal, **13-14**
potatoes, 17
prairie dogs, 39
Prairies, 33
prime minister, 26
Prince Edward Island, **16-17**
Prince of Wales Museum, 58
Privateers' Warehouse, 13
ptarmigan, 63
puffin, **10**
pump-jack, 43

Q

Quebec, **21-24**
Quebec City, **22-23**

R

railway, 40
Red Bay, 10
Red River, 33, **34-35**
red-winged blackbirds, 36
Regina, **38**
Reid, Bill, 27
Richard, Rocket, 28
Rideau Canal, 27
Riding Mountain National Park, **36**
River Walk, 33
Rocher Percé, 21
Rocky Mountains, **43-44**
Rogers Pass, 46, 51
Royal BC Museum, **49-50**
Royal Canadian Mint, **34**
Royal Canadian Mounted Police (RCMP), 38, 40
Royal Ontario Museum (ROM), 29
Royal Tyrrell Museum, 41

S

Saint John River, 19
Saint Lawrence River, **22**, 30
sand, red, 17
sandpiper birds, 20
Saskatchewan, **38-40**
scallops, 13
Science North museum, 31
scurvy, 14
sea otter, 48
sea star, 50
Service, Robert, 55
Signal Hill, 8
smoked meat, 23
SS *Klondike*, 52
St. Boniface, 33
St. John's, **8-9**
Stanley Cup, 29
Stanley Park, 48
stern-wheeler, 52
Sudbury, 31

T

Tadoussac, 22
terns, 20
Terry Fox, **32**
throat singing, 62
tides, 18
Tomb of the Unknown Soldier, 28
Toronto, **28-29**
totem pole, 48
Trans-Canada Highway, 46, 47, 50
tundra, 63

U

United Empire Loyalists, 19-20

V

Vancouver, **48**
Vancouver, George Captain, 50
Vancouver Aquarium, 48
Vancouver Island, 49
Vancouver SkyTrain, 48
Victoria, **49-50**
voyageurs, **37**

W

Wascana Lake, 38
Watson Lake signpost forest, 52
Wawa, 31
West Edmonton Mall, 43
whaling, 10, 22
wheat, 33
Whistler, **48**
Whitehorse, **52-53**
Wildcat Café, 58
windmills, 42
Winnipeg, **33-34**, 35

Y

yellow-headed blackbirds, 35
Yellowknife, **58-59**
Yukon, **52-55**
Yukon River, 52, 53

Z

ziplining, 42